Ankita Rossi

Oder-Neiße Radweg (Oder–Neisse Line Cycle Path)

Title: Oder-Neiße Radweg (Oder–Neisse Line Cycle Path)
Author: Ankita Rossi
Published by: NEXTUNICORN PUBLISHER PROPRIETORSHIP
Publisher's Address: Shree Dwarkadhish Ji Ka Was, Emri, Rajsamand, RAJASTHAN, India. Pincode: 313342
Printer Details: Published online on various platforms.
Edition: 01
ISBN: 978-81-968306-6-3

Images Source: Pixbay: (https://pixabay.com/)

Disclaimer: The author and publisher disclaim all liability for accuracy, loss, or damage arising from the use of this travel guide; users are urged to independently verify information and prioritize personal safety.

Catalog

Welcome to the Travel Guide for the Oder-Neiße Radweg!

Embark on a captivating cultural odyssey as you venture along the Oder-Neiße Line Cycle Path, where history seamlessly intertwines with natural beauty. This picturesque route invites cyclists to delve into the rich tapestry of culture woven into the landscapes it traverses.

Prepare to be transported back in time as you pedal through cities and towns that exude an air of nostalgia. Görlitz, with its well-preserved medieval architecture, offers a journey through the ages. Discover the intricacies of St. Peter and Paul's Church, wander through the historic Old Town, and immerse yourself in the unique atmosphere that embraces this city's heritage.

Frankfurt (Oder), a city that effortlessly blends historical charm with modern vibrancy, awaits your exploration. Marvel at the impressive St. Marienkirche, cross the picturesque bridge connecting Germany and Poland on your bike, and soak up the cultural nuances that make this city an enthralling stop along your route.

Küstrin-Kietz, situated at the confluence of the Oder and Neiße rivers, is a living testament to resilience and transformation. Uncover remnants of Küstrin Fortress, witness historical architecture come alive before your eyes, and immerse yourself in the captivating ambiance shaped by centuries of history.

But don't just limit yourself to well-known landmarks; there are hidden cultural treasures waiting to be discovered along this remarkable cycle path. Delight in quaint villages brimming with local artisans showcasing their traditional crafts. From centuries-old churches to charming market squares, each pedal stroke reveals new cultural delights that will leave you enchanted.

As you embark on your cycling adventure along this majestic path, indulge in gastronomic delights that will energize both body and soul. Local eateries offer a tantalizing array of regional specialties - from savory pierogi in Poland to hearty German stews. Immerse yourself in the unique blend of flavors that define each stop, creating a culinary map of your unforgettable journey.

Prepare to be captivated by the scenic landscapes that unfold before your eyes as you pedal through the Oder-Neiße region. Tranquil riverbanks, verdant meadows, and dense forests paint a breathtaking picture at every turn. Allow yourself to pause at idyllic spots along the riverside, inhaling the fresh air and immersing yourself in the natural beauty that defines this cycling path.

From historical echoes to delectable culinary delights, the Oder-Neiße Radweg beckons cyclists to embark on an extraordinary adventure through diverse cultures and awe-inspiring landscapes. Get ready to pedal through history, savor authentic local flavors, and uncover hidden gems scattered along this enchanting cycle path.

1. Görlitz, Germany

Görlitz, a city with a captivating past, was established in the 12th century and flourished as a bustling medieval trading center. Its architectural marvels, showcasing Gothic, Renaissance, and Baroque influences, offer a glimpse into its rich history.

There are several key attractions that make Görlitz an enchanting destination. The St. Peter and Paul's Church stands as a testament to the city's religious heritage. The historic Old Town boasts an impressive collection of more than 4,000 cultural monuments that take you on a journey through time. And who can forget the iconic City Hall, which adds to the charm of this remarkable place.

To make the most of your visit, it is recommended to plan your trip between May and September when the weather is pleasant and vibrant festivals bring the city to life. Keep in mind that opening hours may vary for each attraction, so it's advisable to check their official websites for accurate information.

If you're looking for hidden gems in Görlitz, look no further than the Via Regia. This ancient trade route winds its way through the city and offers delightful surprises at every turn. Take your time exploring this route and uncovering its charming hidden corners.

Food enthusiasts will be delighted by Görlitz's culinary delights. Don't miss out on trying Silesian Streuselkuchen (crumb cake) at local bakeries - it's a true treat for your taste buds! Additionally, indulge in regional specialties served in traditional restaurants to fully experience the local flavors.

For any inquiries or further information about Görlitz, you can contact them at +49 3581 67-1030 or visit their [Official Website](https://www.goerlitz.de). So pack your bags and embark on an unforgettable adventure in this captivating city!

---

2. Frankfurt (Oder), Germany

Frankfurt (Oder) has a rich history that dates back to the Middle Ages, making it an important trade hub. A testament to its historical significance is St. Marienkirche, a church that was founded in the 13th century.

When visiting Frankfurt (Oder), there are several key attractions worth exploring. These include St. Marienkirche, the Slavic

Fortified Settlement, and the international bridge that connects Germany and Poland.

For those planning a visit, the best time to go is between June and August when the weather is pleasant and cultural events are held.

If you plan on visiting St. Marienkirche, take note of their opening hours: they are open from Monday to Saturday from 10 AM to 4 PM, and on Sundays from 12 PM to 4 PM.

For more information or inquiries, you can contact them at +49 335 553094 or visit their [Official Website](https://www.frankfurt-oder.de).

A hidden gem in Frankfurt (Oder) is the Kleist Museum, which is dedicated to the renowned poet Heinrich von Kleist. It's definitely worth exploring if you have an interest in literature and history.

When it comes to culinary delights in Frankfurt (Oder), make sure to indulge in local specialties such as Spreewald gherkins and traditional German dishes. These flavors will truly enhance your experience of this vibrant city.

---

3. Szczecin, Poland

Szczecin has a rich history that dates back to the 8th century. It has transformed into a significant Baltic seaport, with a city that has experienced its fair share of ups and downs.

If you're planning to visit Szczecin, make sure to check out some of its key attractions. The Szczecin Castle, Wały Chrobrego Promenade, and the National Museum are definitely worth exploring.

For the best weather and outdoor events, it's recommended to visit Szczecin between May and September. This period offers milder temperatures and plenty of opportunities to enjoy outdoor activities.

If you're interested in visiting the Szczecin Castle, take note of its opening hours. It is open from Tuesday to Sunday, from 10 AM to 4 PM.

To get in touch with them or gather more information, you can contact them at +48 91 430 24 40 or visit their [Official Website](https://www.zamek.szczecin.pl).

One hidden gem in Szczecin is exploring the Waly Chrobrego at sunset. This will reward you with breathtaking views of the Oder River that you won't want to miss.

When it comes to culinary delights, don't forget to try local seafood dishes at the bustling Hakenterrasse. It's a great place to indulge in delicious seafood while soaking up the vibrant atmosphere.

So if you're looking for an intriguing city with a fascinating past and exciting attractions, consider adding Szczecin to your travel itinerary.

Międzyzdroje, a charming coastal destination with a rich history dating back to the 19th century, has garnered acclaim as a beloved seaside resort boasting pristine sandy beaches. When planning your visit to this enchanting town, be sure to check out its key attractions, including the iconic Międzyzdroje Pier, where you can take leisurely strolls and soak in breathtaking views of the shoreline. Another highlight is the Walk of Fame, which pays homage to renowned personalities who have graced this picturesque locale. Additionally, don't miss out on the annual Film Festival that takes place during the months of June to September, offering a fantastic blend of cinematic delights and beachside activities.

For those seeking an immersive experience in nature's embrace, venture into the hidden gem that is Wolin National Park. This tranquil haven showcases awe-inspiring natural landscapes that will leave you in awe.

To satisfy your taste buds with delectable delights, make sure to indulge in the culinary offerings available at local beachfront restaurants. Here, you can savor an array of fresh seafood dishes that will tantalize your palate and leave you craving for more.

When planning your itinerary for Międzyzdroje Pier specifically, keep in mind that it operates from 9 AM to 9 PM daily - perfect for enjoying all it has to offer at any time during the day.

For further information or inquiries about Międzyzdroje and its attractions, feel free to contact +48 91 328 24 43 or visit their [Official Website](https://www.miedzyzdroje.pl).

---

5. Wolin, Poland

Wolin has a rich history that goes back to the early medieval period, making it a thriving hub for trade and craftsmanship. It offers a range of key attractions, including the Wolin Open-Air Museum, Wolin National Park, and the reconstructed Wolin stronghold. To make the most of your visit, it is recommended to plan your trip between May and October when you can enjoy outdoor activities and historical events. The Wolin Open-Air Museum operates from 9 AM to 6 PM daily. If you need any further information, you can contact them at +48 91 323 60 66 or visit their official website at http://www.wolinpn.pl. A hidden gem in Wolin is its tranquil beaches on Wolin Island, perfect for exploration. Additionally, don't miss out on trying local delicacies at the charming village taverns for an authentic culinary experience.

When it comes to the history of Świnoujście, we can trace its maritime roots all the way back to the Middle Ages. Its strategic location on the Baltic Sea has played a significant role in shaping its past.

If you're looking for key attractions in Świnoujście, be sure to check out Baltic Park, Gerhard's Fort, and take a leisurely stroll along the seaside promenade. These spots offer unique experiences that showcase the beauty and charm of this coastal town.

For those planning a visit, June to August is an ideal time as it offers both beach activities and a vibrant atmosphere. The summer months bring life to the town, making it a perfect destination for fun under the sun.

If you're interested in exploring Gerhard's Fort, note that it operates from Tuesday to Sunday between 10 AM and 4 PM. It's worth paying a visit to delve into its historical significance.

Should you need any further information or wish to contact them directly, feel free to reach out at +48 91 322 21 77 or visit their official website [here](https://www.swinoujscie.pl). They will be more than happy to assist you with any inquiries.

Now, let me share with you a hidden gem in Świnoujście - the Museum of Sea Fishery. This fascinating attraction offers an insight into the rich maritime history of the area. It's definitely worth adding this stop to your itinerary if you want to delve deeper into Świnoujście's past.

Lastly, don't miss out on indulging in culinary delights while visiting this coastal town. Local seafood restaurants offer an array of fresh fish dishes that are sure to tantalize your taste buds. It's an opportunity not only for delicious meals but also for experiencing the flavors unique to this region.

---

7. Wolgast, Germany

Wolgast, with its medieval origins, has a rich history as the residence of the dukes of Pomerania. When exploring this charming town, make sure to visit key attractions such as the St. Petri Church, the iconic Peene Bridge, and the historic Old Town.

For the best experience, plan your visit between May and September when the weather is pleasant and perfect for outdoor exploration. The St. Petri Church is open daily from 9 AM to 5 PM.

To get in touch or gather more information about Wolgast, you can contact them at +49 3836 205123 or visit their official website at [Official Website](https://www.wolgast.de).
If you're looking for a hidden gem in Wolgast, don't miss out on exploring the Peenemünde Historical Technical Museum.
When it comes to culinary delights, indulge in local fish specialties at waterfront restaurants for a truly unforgettable experience.
---

8. Zielona Góra, Poland

Zielona Góra, a city with a rich history dating back to the 13th century, gained prominence during the Middle Ages for its viticulture. This charming destination offers a range of key attractions worth exploring, including the Palm House, Piast Tower, and the Old Town. For those planning a visit, it is recommended to come between April and October when outdoor activities and cultural events are in full swing. The Palm House is open from Tuesday to Sunday, welcoming visitors from 10 AM to 6 PM. If you need any further information or assistance, you can reach out at +48 68 328 26 20 or visit the official website at [Official Website](https://www.zielona-gora.pl). While exploring Zielona Góra, don't miss out on discovering the hidden gem of

Lubuskie Vineyards where you can indulge in tasting local wines. To truly savor the essence of this region, make sure to try traditional Lubuskie cuisine at local restaurants for an unforgettable culinary experience.

---

9. Gubin, Poland

Gubin, with its medieval origins, holds a rich history shaped by various significant events due to its strategic location. It boasts several key attractions that draw visitors, including the impressive Gubin Castle, the Parish Church of St. James, and the Lusatian Culture Center. To make the most of your visit, it is recommended to plan your trip between May and September when you can enjoy outdoor exploration and immerse yourself in cultural festivals.

If you're interested in exploring Gubin Castle, be sure to take note of its opening hours from Tuesday to Sunday, 9 AM to 5 PM. For any inquiries or further information about Gubin, you can contact them at +48 68 385 22 06 or visit their [Official Website](https://www.gubin.pl).

One hidden gem worth discovering is the picturesque Gubin Landscape Park, where you can embark on scenic nature walks and appreciate the beauty of the natural surroundings.

When it comes to culinary delights, don't miss out on trying local Lusatian specialties in the charming Old Town area. It's a wonderful opportunity to savor unique flavors and indulge in gastronomic experiences that showcase the region's distinctive cuisine.

In conclusion, Gubin offers a captivating blend of history, culture, and natural beauty that will leave visitors with lasting memories. Plan your visit accordingly and make sure to explore all that this enchanting destination has to offer.

---

10. Cottbus, Germany

Cottbus, with its medieval origins, has flourished as a bustling hub for trade and textiles. When visiting this charming town, be sure to check out some of its key attractions such as the picturesque Branitz Park, the historic St. Nicholas' Church, and the captivating performances at the State Theatre. To make the most of your trip, plan to visit between May and September when you can enjoy outdoor activities and immerse yourself in cultural events. Branitz

Park welcomes visitors from 8 AM to 8 PM daily, offering a delightful escape into nature. For further information or inquiries, you can contact +49 355 75150 or visit their [Official Website](https://www.cottbus.de). As you explore Cottbus, don't miss out on the hidden gem that is the Wendish Museum, where you can gain fascinating insights into regional history. And of course, indulge in culinary delights by savoring local specialties at traditional German restaurants.

---

11. Spreewald Biosphere Reserve, Germany

The Spreewald region holds a captivating past that dates back to the medieval era, molded by its exceptional waterways. If you're planning a visit, there are several noteworthy attractions to explore. Embark on boat tours that navigate the intricate canals, immerse yourself in the rich history showcased at the Lehde Open-Air Museum, and bask in the charm of the picturesque village of Lübbenau. For optimal weather and outdoor activities, it is recommended to visit between May and September. Keep in mind that opening hours may vary for each attraction, so it's advisable to check their respective official websites or contact them at +49 3542 2287. As you traverse this remarkable region, don't miss out on the hidden gem of the Peitz Prison Museum, which offers a unique historical perspective. And when it comes to satisfying your taste buds, be sure to try the famous Spreewald pickles and indulge in traditional Sorbian cuisine for an authentic culinary experience.

---

12. Muskau Park, Germany/Poland

One of the most fascinating historical sites to explore is Muskau Park, which was created by Prince Pückler-Muskau in the 19th century. This cross-border gem is even listed as a UNESCO masterpiece. When you visit, be prepared to be captivated by the key attractions such as Muskau Castle, the iconic Rakotzbrücke Devil's Bridge, and the meticulously landscaped gardens. To fully experience the beauty of the park, it's best to plan your visit between April and October when the gardens are in full bloom and outdoor exploration is at its finest. Muskau Castle welcomes visitors from Tuesday to Sunday from 10 AM to 5 PM, so make sure to plan your day accordingly. If you need any additional information or have any inquiries, you can contact them at +49 3571 6030 or visit their official website [here](https://www.pueckler-museum.de). As you wander through this enchanting place, don't miss out on discovering one of its hidden gems – the unique architecture of the artificial Ruins of the Red Castle. And when it's time for a culinary delight, why not enjoy a delightful picnic within the park or venture into the charming town of Bad Muskau for a memorable dining experience? With its rich blend of historical significance, cultural treasures, and natural wonders along the Oder-Neiße Radweg, these destinations offer an extraordinary journey that will leave you enchanted every step of the way.

Here's what you need to know before embarking on the Oder-Neiße Radweg:

Currency:
- The official currency used along the Oder-Neiße Radweg is the Euro (€).

Language:
- The primary language spoken in different regions along the Oder-Neiße Radweg may vary. While English is commonly understood in popular tourist areas, it's beneficial to learn a few basic phrases in the local language, whether it's German or Polish. This will enhance your interaction with locals and enrich your travel experience.

Emergency Numbers:
- In case of emergencies along the Oder-Neiße Radweg, it's important to remember these vital contact numbers:
  - Ambulance: 112
  - Police: 110
  - Fire: 112
- When calling from outside the region, make sure to dial your international access code followed by the country code and then the local number.

Useful Websites:
- While cycling along the Oder-Neiße Radweg, there are some online resources that can be beneficial:
  - RadwegInfo (www.radweginfo.com): This website provides official cycle path information including maps and route details.
  - Local Accommodations: Explore regional options for a comfortable stay.
  - Culinary Experiences: Discover local flavors and dining options.

Daily Costs:
Budget (Less than €50):
If you're on a budget, there are affordable options available along the Oder-Neiße Radweg. Hostel dorm beds typically range from €15 to €30, while budget guesthouses offer double rooms from

€40 to €80. You can also find economical meal choices at local eateries with prices for snacks and meals ranging from €5 to €15.

Midrange (€50–€150):

For a more comfortable experience, midrange options are available along the Oder-Neiße Radweg that offer good value. Double rooms in midrange accommodations typically cost between €80 and €120. You can enjoy local cuisine at restaurants, with meal prices ranging from €15 to €40 per person.

Top End (More than €150):

Travelers seeking premium experiences will find upscale options along the Oder-Neiße Radweg. Four- or five-star hotels offer double rooms from €120 to €250. Indulge in gourmet dining experiences at top-end restaurants, with prices per person ranging from €40 to €100.

Opening Hours:

Opening hours along the Oder-Neiße Radweg can vary depending on the season. Generally, businesses operate during high seasons (Apr–Sep/Oct) with reduced hours during shoulder and low seasons. Here are some key times to keep in mind:

- Bike Rental Shops: Open from 9 AM to 6 PM daily.
- Restaurants and Cafes: Opening times vary by location but are typically from 8 AM to 10 PM.
- Local Shops: Open from 9 AM to 7 PM, Monday to Saturday.

Arriving along the Oder-Neiße Radweg:

Depending on your starting point along the Oder-Neiße Radweg, you'll likely arrive at key access points. Here are transportation options available from major entry points to key destinations:

- Frankfurt (Oder), Germany: Trains and buses are available for further travel.
- Szczecin, Poland: Well-connected by trains and buses for onward journeys.
- Görlitz, Germany: Accessible via trains and buses that connect to the larger network.
- Zittau, Germany: Regional transportation options are available for onward travel.

With these essential details in mind, cyclists can embark on the Oder-Neiße Radweg well-prepared, embracing the natural beauty, cultural richness, and exciting cycling adventures along the route.

Itineraries

Embark on a captivating cycling adventure along the Oder-Neiße Radweg for a duration of 2 weeks. Let's dive into the detailed itinerary, ensuring that each day is filled with excitement and discovery.

Days 1 - 3: Görlitz, Germany

Our journey begins in the well-preserved medieval town of Görlitz. Here, you'll be captivated by the harmonious blend of architectural styles spanning centuries. Immerse yourself in the rich history of this charming starting point and marvel at its timeless beauty.

Days 4 - 6: Frankfurt (Oder), Germany

Cycle through the historic streets of Frankfurt (Oder) and prepare to be enchanted by St. Marienkirche, a magnificent church that holds stories from the past. As you cross the bridge connecting Germany and Poland, symbolizing unity, you'll witness firsthand the unique cultural blend of this border town.

Days 7 - 9: Szczecin, Poland

Pedal your way into Szczecin, a bustling port city known for its maritime heritage and vibrant cultural scene. Explore historic landmarks such as the castle and immerse yourself in the dynamic atmosphere that this Polish gem has to offer.

Days 10 - 12: Miedzyzdroje, Poland

Take some time to relax on the sandy beaches of Miedzyzdroje while exploring this bustling resort town known for its iconic pier and annual film festival. Dive into its maritime charm and experience firsthand its seaside allure along our picturesque cycle path.

Days 13 - 15: Wolin, Poland

Transport yourself back in time as we arrive at Wolin, an island town boasting a reconstructed medieval stronghold. Discover hidden treasures within Wolin National Park and bear witness to the historical legacy that makes this destination truly special along our Oder-Neiße Radweg adventure.

Days 16 - 18: Świnoujście, Poland

Prepare to be amazed by the vibrant seaside resort city of Świnoujście. Explore historic forts, admire lighthouses, and immerse yourself in the stunning beauty of Swinoujscie Baltic Park. Allow the coastal atmosphere to captivate your senses as we continue our journey through this Polish coastal gem.

Days 19 - 21: Zielona Góra, Poland

Our final destination is Zielona Góra, where we will explore the wine culture that characterizes this region. Known for its vineyards and historic Old Town, indulge in the culinary experiences that await you in this unique Polish city.

As you can see, this carefully curated cycling itinerary along the Oder-Neiße Radweg promises a harmonious blend of history, culture, and natural beauty. It offers cyclists a truly unique and enriching journey through the heart of Central Europe.

Off the Beaten Path Discovery - 2 Weeks

For those seeking hidden gems and cultural treasures along lesser-explored routes of the Oder-Neiße Radweg, we have a special discovery itinerary that will leave you spellbound.

Days 1 - 3: Gubin, Poland

Crossing over the Neiße River brings us to Gubin – a town steeped in historical architecture and rich cultural heritage. Meander through its charming streets while uncovering captivating stories embedded within every corner.

Days 4 - 6: Cottbus, Germany

Delve into Cottbus – a vibrant university city brimming with parks, theaters, and historic landmarks. Visit Branitz Park and St. Nicholas' Church while savoring local specialties at traditional German restaurants for an authentic taste of this delightful region.

Days 7 - 9: Spreewald Biosphere Reserve Germany

Immerse yourself in the lush waterways and unique flora of the Spreewald Biosphere Reserve, a UNESCO-listed site. Enjoy serene boat tours, explore the Lehde Open-Air Museum, and indulge in the natural beauty that envelops this enchanting region.

Days 10 - 12: Muskau Park Germany/Poland

Cycle through the cross-border UNESCO-listed Muskau Park, a masterpiece created by Prince Pückler-Muskau in the 19th century. Marvel at the iconic Rakotzbrücke Devil's Bridge and appreciate the extensive landscaped gardens that showcase true artistry.

Days 13 - 15: Zittau, Germany

Conclude your off-the-beaten-path journey in Zittau — a town that offers regional transportation options for your convenience. Take a moment to reflect on the diverse landscapes and cultural richness you have experienced throughout this lesser-known segment of the Oder-Neiße Radweg.

With this extraordinary itinerary, you will uncover hidden treasures and embark on an adventure filled with discovery along our remarkable Oder-Neiße Radweg route.

Embark on a captivating hiking expedition through the enchanting Oder-Neiße Radweg, where picturesque trails and historical landscapes await your exploration.

Hiking

Görlitz Hills:
Unveil the breathtaking natural allure of the Görlitz Hills, boasting panoramic vistas that seamlessly blend historical charm with rolling landscapes.
Neiße River Walk:

Indulge in a leisurely stroll along the meandering Neiße River, as you discover hidden paths and scenic spots that immerse you in the tranquil embrace of nature's embrace.

Cycling Adventures

For cycling enthusiasts, the Oder-Neiße Radweg offers a plethora of exhilarating possibilities to revel in the scenic beauty of the region.

Gubin to Frankfurt (Oder):
Pedal your way through a tapestry of cultural richness as you journey from Gubin to Frankfurt (Oder), exploring charming towns and savoring picturesque landscapes along the way.

Oder Valley Trail:
Embark on an awe-inspiring cycling expedition along the Oder Valley Trail, where you'll witness ever-changing scenery that captures the very essence of this majestic river's journey through diverse terrains.

Water-Based Excitement

Immerse yourself in a realm of water-based excitement as you explore alluring aquatic activities along the Oder-Neiße Radweg, where rivers and lakes become your playground for adventure.

Neiße River Canoeing:
Embark on a thrilling canoeing escapade down the meandering Neiße River, navigating through lush landscapes and encountering nature's wonders at every turn.

Lake District Exploration:
Uncover hidden gems in the form of serene lakes dotted along your route. Whether it's kayaking or enjoying a peaceful lakeside picnic, these tranquil oases add an invigorating touch to your cycling odyssey.

Nature-Inspired Challenges

For those seeking an adrenaline rush, the Oder-Neiße Radweg presents a host of nature-inspired challenges to test your mettle.
Rock Climbing in Zittau:
Push yourself to new heights with an exhilarating rock climbing adventure in Zittau. Whether you're a beginner or an experienced

climber, the cliffs offer thrilling routes that will leave you feeling accomplished.

Sailing on Lake Berzdorf:
Feel the wind in your hair and embrace the freedom of open waters as you sail across Lake Berzdorf. Surrounded by awe-inspiring landscapes, this experience promises pure bliss and excitement.

Best Times to Embark

- Spring (April to June):
 Springtime unveils a captivating tapestry of blooming wildflowers and moderate temperatures along the Oder-Neiße Radweg, making it an ideal season for hiking and cycling adventures.
- Summer (July and September):
 Escape the crowds and bask in the glory of water-based activities during summer. Canoeing and lakeside exploration are at their finest during this time, allowing you to fully immerse yourself in nature's wonders.
- Winter (December to March):
 While winter may limit some outdoor activities along the Oder-Neiße Radweg, it presents a unique opportunity for unforgettable experiences like winter hiking. Discover the serene beauty of the landscape as it transforms into a winter wonderland.
Embark on an enchanting journey along the Oder-Neiße Radweg, where nature's wonders intertwine with thrilling adventures to create memories that will last a lifetime.

The Oder-Neiße Radweg, also known as the Oder–Neisse Line Cycle Path, has its origins in the geopolitical changes that occurred in Central Europe during the mid-20th century. This cycle path's historical narrative is closely tied to the post-World War II landscape and the reconfiguration of borders.

In the aftermath of World War II, Europe underwent significant political restructuring through events like the Yalta and Potsdam Conferences. The Oder-Neiße Line, which was drawn along the Oder and Neiße Rivers, played a crucial role in this reconfiguration. It served as Germany's eastern boundary according to an agreement made by Allied Powers such as the Soviet Union, United States, and United Kingdom. As a result, there were substantial territorial shifts.

The implementation of the Oder-Neiße Line led to significant changes in the region's geography. Populations were expelled and resettled as areas east of the line, including Stettin (now Szczecin), were ceded to Poland. The Neiße River became a natural border separating Germany and Poland.

Therefore, the Oder-Neiße Radweg follows these historic rivers' course and takes cyclists through landscapes that bear witness to these geopolitical transformations. The cycle path serves as a conduit for exploring both natural and cultural heritage shaped by mid-20th century events. Cyclists embarking on this journey engage with a geographic tapestry that reflects post-war history's intricacies, making it a unique and historically charged experience. The development of the Oder-Neiße Radweg from a geopolitical boundary to a celebrated cycle path involved collaborative efforts between German and Polish authorities. These efforts aimed not only to create a recreational route but also to foster cross-border cooperation while promoting understanding and appreciation of shared history and cultural diversity in the region.

As cyclists traverse through this route, they encounter various cultural heritage sites that reflect the intertwined histories of Germany and Poland. Historic towns like Görlitz and Zittau showcase architectural gems from different eras, highlighting the diverse cultural influences that have shaped the region.

The cycle path intentionally intersects with historical landmarks, serving as a living testament to the preservation of memory. Cyclists may find themselves passing through areas that were once part of the German Democratic Republic, experiencing tangible remnants of a bygone era.

Moreover, the Oder-Neiße Radweg often aligns with cultural events and festivals that celebrate the shared heritage of the region. These occasions provide opportunities for locals and visitors to engage in cultural exchange, fostering unity and mutual appreciation.

Planning a cycling adventure along the Oder-Neiße Radweg involves more than just enjoying the beautiful scenery. It's important to choose accommodations that suit your preferences and budget. Here's a comprehensive guide to help you find the perfect place to stay, with indicative price ranges for each option.

1. Booking Strategies for Optimal Stays:

To ensure a smooth trip along the Oder-Neiße Radweg, it's advisable to plan ahead and book in advance. While this route may not be as crowded as coastal areas, it's still wise to secure your accommodations, especially during peak times or significant events. Prices can vary, but expect a range of €40 to €80 per night for standard accommodations.

2. Seasonal Nuances and Planning:

Understanding the seasonal patterns along the Oder-Neiße Radweg is crucial for budgeting and planning your trip effectively. It's best to align your journey with favorable weather conditions and avoid potential crowds. Prices may fluctuate depending on the season, so budget around €50 to €90 per night during peak times and potentially lower rates of €40 to €70 during quieter periods.

3. Cost Variances Across Regions:

Similar to Italy, accommodation prices can vary across different regions along the Oder-Neiße Radweg. A charming lodging in a rural setting might have a different pricing structure compared to a similar option in a historic town. Expect regional variations with budget options ranging from €45 to €80 and midrange choices averaging €70 to €120.

4. Unique Stay Options Along the Path:

One of the highlights of cycling along the Oder-Neiße Radweg is exploring the diverse range of accommodations available. From cozy bed and breakfasts (B&Bs) to rustic farm stays, there are plenty of options that cater to different budgets and preferences. Budget around €40 to €80 for B&Bs and farm stays, with prices varying based on amenities and location. Mountain huts can also provide budget-friendly options, ranging from €25 to €40 per person.

5. Hidden Gems: Convents and Monasteries:

For a unique cultural experience at an affordable price, consider staying in a convent or monastery along the Oder-Neiße Radweg. Prices for these accommodations typically range from €30 to €60 per night. While some may have specific requirements or restrictions, exploring these historic abodes can offer a serene and enriching overnight experience.

6. Campgrounds: Nature's Resting Spots:

Camping enthusiasts will find plenty of affordable options along the Oder-Neiße Radweg. Prices at campgrounds can vary depending on the season, ranging from €10 to €25 per adult. Some campgrounds offer all-inclusive prices, while others charge separately for different aspects of your stay. Budget-conscious travelers can enjoy picturesque camping spots without overspending.

7. Mountain Huts for Alpine Retreats:

For those seeking an authentic alpine experience reminiscent of Italy's rifugi, mountain huts along the Oder-Neiße Radweg are a great option. Prices range from €20 to €30 per person and may include breakfast. It's important to book in advance as these huts offer panoramic views and a sense of camaraderie among fellow cyclists.

8. Cultural Exchange at Hostels:

Hostels along the Oder-Neiße Radweg serve as hubs for cultural exchange among travelers. Prices for dormitory beds typically range from €20 to €40 per night, with variations based on location and amenities offered by each hostel. Some hostels may provide additional services such as meals for an extra cost, while private rooms might be available at slightly higher rates.

9.Villas for Scenic Retreats:

If you're looking to indulge in luxurious comfort amidst historical and natural wonders, villa rentals along the Oder-Neiße Radweg are worth considering. Prices for villas can vary widely, with budget-friendly options starting from €80 to €150 per night. For more opulent choices or larger groups, expect rates of €150 to

€300 or more per night. Agencies specializing in villa rentals offer a range of choices to suit different preferences and budgets.
By following these guidelines, you can ensure a memorable and comfortable stay along the Oder-Neiße Radweg without breaking the bank. Happy cycling!

Planning a cycling adventure along the Oder-Neiße Radweg? It's essential to have a good grasp of the visa and residency requirements. Let me guide you through the legal aspects of your journey with this comprehensive information:

1. Schengen Treaty Implications:

If you're a European citizen from a country in the Schengen Treaty, you won't need a visa to cycle through the Oder-Neiße Radweg. Simply carry a valid identity card or passport for entry.

2. Visa Exemptions for Selected Countries:

Visitors from non-EU countries like Australia, Canada, Japan, and the USA enjoy visa exemptions for tourist visits of up to 90 days. However, it's crucial to check specific requirements based on your nationality.

3. Non-EU and Non-Schengen Nationals:

Travelers from non-EU and non-Schengen countries who plan on cycling for more than 90 days or have purposes other than tourism (such as work or study) might need specific visas. To get precise and updated information, visit www.esteri.it/visti/home_eng.asp or contact the relevant Italian consulate.

4. Residency and Work for EU Citizens:

EU citizens cycling along the Oder-Neiße Radweg do not require permits for short stays. However, if you plan on residing for more than three months, make sure to register at the local municipal registry office. You may also need to provide proof of work or financial means.

5. Permanent Residence for Non-EU Foreign Citizens:

Non-EU citizens who have legally resided in Italy continuously for five years (even while cycling) can apply for permanent residency.

6. 'Permesso di Soggiorno' (Permit to Stay):

For non-EU citizens planning an extended stay along the Oder-Neiße Radweg, it's important to obtain a 'permesso di soggiorno' from the local police station. Tourists staying in hotels are usually exempt from this requirement. However, if you're planning on studying, working, or staying for an extended period, you'll need a 'permesso di soggiorno,' which can be obtained from the police. EU citizens are exempt from this requirement.

7. Study Visas:

If you're a non-EU citizen planning to study along the Oder-Neiße Radweg and fully immerse yourself in the local culture, you'll need to apply for a study visa at the nearest Italian embassy or consulate. The application typically requires proof of enrollment, fee payment, and financial means to sustain yourself during your study period.

By understanding these visa and residency intricacies, your cycling journey along the Oder-Neiße Radweg will be both legally compliant and enjoyable. Always refer to official sources for the latest updates to ensure a seamless travel experience.

Embarking on the Oder-Neiße Radweg guarantees an exhilarating cycling adventure through a variety of landscapes. Throughout the seasons, this picturesque cycle path reveals its unique wonders. Let's explore the seasonal highlights along this captivating route:

Spring (March to May):

- A Symphony of Flowers: Nature awakens, painting vibrant flowers across the landscapes. The meadows burst with an array of colors, creating a visual symphony that delights nature enthusiasts and photographers alike.

- Mild Temperatures: Spring brings along comfortable weather, making it an ideal time for a leisurely ride.

Summer (June to August):

- Long Days and Warm Nights: Immerse yourself in the charm of long summer days along the Oder-Neiße Radweg. With extended daylight hours, you'll have ample time for exploration, while warm evenings invite relaxation by the tranquil riverbanks.

- Festivals and Local Events: Along this route, many towns host vibrant summer festivals that offer a cultural immersion. Indulge in local music, cuisine, and traditions to add a festive touch to your cycling journey.

Autumn (September to November):

- A Spectacle of Foliage: As autumn unfolds its magic, behold the breathtaking transformation of foliage along the cycle path. Pedal through corridors adorned with red, gold, and orange leaves to experience an enchanting ambiance.

- Harvest Vibes: Discover local markets en route and savor autumn's bounty. From freshly harvested fruits to regional specialties, indulge in culinary delights that perfectly align with the season.

Winter (December to February):

- Serenity Unveiled: While winter may not be considered peak cycling season, it reveals a serene side of the Oder-Neiße Radweg.

Snow-capped landscapes and frozen rivers create a tranquil atmosphere that captivates all who venture forth.

- Cozy Villages: Take refuge in cozy villages along the way. Embrace the quietude of winter, explore historical sites, and relish in hearty local dishes that warm the soul.

Year-Round Attractions:

- Historical Gems: Throughout the Oder-Neiße Radweg, historical treasures await discovery. Regardless of the season, immerse yourself in the rich cultural heritage found within castles, churches, and charming villages.

- Seasonal Gastronomy: Delight in regional specialties that change with each passing season. From bountiful fresh produce during summer to heartwarming stews during winter, every bite tells a story of local culinary traditions.

- Scenic River Views: The Oder and Neiße rivers provide a constant scenic backdrop along your journey. Capture awe-inspiring river views framed by blossoming flowers in spring, vibrant autumn leaves, or a tranquil blanket of snow.

Remember to choose the time that aligns with your preferences and desires along the Oder-Neiße Radweg. Whether you seek the burst of life during spring, embrace the warmth of summer, immerse yourself in autumn's hues, or revel in winter's tranquility - each season offers its own unique charm.

Embarking on the Oder-Neiße Radweg offers an enchanting cycling experience through diverse landscapes. To ensure a seamless adventure, let's break down the route into manageable sections, highlighting key landmarks, towns, and scenic spots, along with essential information about elevation profiles and difficulty ratings.

Section 1: Zittau to Görlitz

Covering a distance of approximately 35 km, this section allows you to start your journey in Zittau, a town steeped in rich cultural heritage. As you cycle through picturesque landscapes and cross the Neiße River, you'll eventually arrive in Görlitz. This town is famed for its well-preserved medieval architecture and promises awe-inspiring sights.

Section 2: Görlitz to Forst

Spanning around 50 km, this section takes you through the enchanting Lusatian Neiße Nature Park. Along the way, you'll pass by the historic town of Rothenburg before reaching Forst. Known for its blend of German and Slavic influences, Forst offers a unique cultural experience. The lush forests surrounding this area provide a serene backdrop for your journey.

Section 3: Forst to Frankfurt (Oder)

Covering approximately 60 km, this section guides you through the Lower Lusatia region with its expansive open landscapes. Your destination is Frankfurt (Oder), a city that seamlessly blends medieval charm with contemporary architecture. As you pedal through the open countryside and alongside the charming Oder River, prepare to be captivated by nature's beauty.

Section 4: Frankfurt (Oder) to Küstrin-Kietz

This section spans roughly 40 km and follows the path along the Oder River. Along the way, you'll pass through Seelow—a place of historical significance—and eventually reach Küstrin-Kietz. Nestled on the banks of the Oder River, Küstrin-Kietz offers a picturesque setting. Take your time to admire the riverine landscapes and explore the Seelow Heights Battlefield.

Section 5: Küstrin-Kietz to Schwedt
With a distance of approximately 65 km, this section takes you through the fertile plains of the Oderbruch region. Eventually, you'll arrive in Schwedt—a town that seamlessly combines industrial history with natural beauty. The expansive views of the Oderbruch and the parks and waterways in Schwedt offer a tranquil escape.

Section 6: Schwedt to Szczecin
Covering around 40 km, this section marks your entry into Poland as you cross the Oder-Neiße border. Your destination is Szczecin— a city known for its maritime heritage and historical sites. Revel in the marvel of where the Oder and Neiße rivers converge while immersing yourself in Szczecin's vibrant cultural offerings.

When it comes to elevation profiles and difficulty ratings, overall terrain along the Oder-Neiße Radweg is predominantly flat to gently rolling, accommodating cyclists of various skill levels. Sections 1 to 3 are generally easy, featuring well-maintained paths. Sections 4 and 5 may pose slightly more challenging terrain due to varied landscapes. Section 6 involves navigating urban areas as you cross into Poland, requiring extra attention.

To ensure a smooth journey, here are some pro tips:
- Navigation: Utilize GPS devices or cycling apps for accurate guidance.
- Services: Plan rest stops in towns for amenities such as cafes, bike repair shops, and accommodations.
- Weather: Stay updated on weather forecasts, especially during transitional seasons.

By following this detailed breakdown, cyclists can effectively plan their Oder-Neiße Radweg adventure while anticipating both cultural highlights and cycling challenges that make this route an unforgettable experience.

Events and Festivals Calendar: Oder-Neiße Radweg

Embarking on a cycling adventure along the Oder-Neiße Radweg not only allows you to soak in the breathtaking landscapes but also immerses you in the vibrant local culture through an array of exciting events and festivals. Take a look at this calendar that highlights noteworthy occasions along the route throughout the year:

Spring: March to May

1. Cherry Blossom Festivals
   - Location: Görlitz and Frankfurt (Oder)
   - Description: Embrace the arrival of spring with delightful cherry blossom festivals, featuring captivating cultural performances, mouthwatering food stalls, and the awe-inspiring beauty of blooming cherry trees.

2. Seelow Heights Battlefield Commemoration
   - Location: Seelow
   - Description: Engage in historical reenactments and moving ceremonies that pay tribute to the Seelow Heights Battlefield, providing valuable insights into the region's wartime history.

Summer: June to August

1. Oderbruch Music Festival
   - Location: Schwedt
   - Description: Indulge in a melodic journey at the Oderbruch Music Festival, where classical masterpieces intertwine with contemporary compositions amidst the stunning backdrop of nature's wonders.

2. Szczecin Summer Open-Air Concerts
   - Location: Szczecin
   - Description: Experience an electrifying atmosphere as open-air concerts echo through Szczecin's historic architecture, showcasing an eclectic mix of musical genres that will leave you enchanted.

3. Cultural Nights in Küstrin-Kietz
   - Location: Küstrin-Kietz

- Description: Immerse yourself in a captivating arts scene during Cultural Nights, where music, dance, and art take center stage in the charming town of Küstrin-Kietz.

Autumn: September to November

1. Harvest Festivals

   - Location: Various towns along the route

   - Description: Celebrate the bountiful autumn harvest at vibrant local festivals, where farmers' markets overflow with fresh produce, traditional delicacies tempt your taste buds, and cultural performances captivate your senses.

2. Szczecin International Film Festival

   - Location: Szczecin

   - Description: Delve into the world of cinema at the Szczecin International Film Festival, where captivating screenings of international and local films add a touch of cinematic magic to your cycling journey.

Winter: December to February

1. Christmas Markets

   - Location: Görlitz, Frankfurt (Oder), Szczecin

   - Description: Immerse yourself in the enchanting ambiance of Christmas markets that adorn Görlitz, Frankfurt (Oder), and Szczecin during winter. Explore stalls adorned with festive decorations, tantalize your taste buds with seasonal treats, and revel in the cozy atmosphere that surrounds you.

2. New Year's Eve Celebrations

   - Location: Various towns along the route

   - Description: Bid farewell to the old year and welcome the new one by joining locals in lively New Year's Eve celebrations filled with dazzling fireworks displays, live music performances, and an array of festive events held in town squares across different towns along the route.

Year-Round: Markets and Local Fairs

1. Weekly Markets

   - Location: Multiple towns along Oder-Neiße Radweg

   - Description: Immerse yourself in local culture by exploring weekly markets that offer a delightful array of fresh produce, artisanal goods crafted with passion, and opportunities to connect with friendly locals who breathe life into these vibrant marketplaces.

2. Craft Fairs and Artisan Markets
   - Location: Rotating locations
   - Description: Uncover the region's rich craftsmanship at various fairs and markets that showcase an exquisite array of handmade products, captivating art exhibitions, and interactive demonstrations that highlight the true essence of local artistry.

This comprehensive events and festivals calendar adds an extra layer of richness to your Oder-Neiße Radweg experience, allowing you to synchronize your cycling journey with the vibrant cultural tapestry that unfolds along the route. So get ready to embark on a memorable adventure filled with captivating moments and unforgettable encounters!

Key Junctions on the Oder-Neiße Radweg

Embarking on a cycling adventure along the Oder-Neiße Radweg presents cyclists with a series of noteworthy junctions that play a vital role in this scenic route. These junctions not only serve as important navigational points but also offer exciting opportunities to discover nearby attractions. Let's delve into these key junctions, each with its own distinct character and captivating surroundings:
1. Starting Point: Zittau, Germany
  - Our journey commences in Zittau, an enchanting town renowned for its exquisite architecture. Cyclists will easily spot the starting point, usually located near the heart of the town or an iconic landmark.
2. Junction 1: Oder-Neiße Confluence
  - This significant juncture marks the convergence of two majestic rivers, the Oder and Neiße. Take a moment to marvel at this picturesque confluence and relish in the breathtaking riverside vistas before continuing your expedition.
3. Junction 2: Görlitz
  - The captivating town of Görlitz is another key milestone along this route, adorned with impeccably preserved medieval structures. Cyclists may choose to immerse themselves in its historical center or venture off on a detour to uncover its cultural treasures.
4. Junction 3: Bridge Crossing to Poland
  - As you cross over into Poland, this junction signifies your international journey ahead. The bridge offers panoramic views of the river landscape, providing a perfect backdrop for memorable moments.
5. Junction 4: Świnoujście
  - Nestled by the coast, Świnoujście acts as a gateway to the Baltic Sea. Take some time to unwind, explore sandy beaches, or indulge in local attractions before resuming your northbound adventure.
6. Junction 5: Ueckermünde

- This scenic town along the route, Ueckermünde, offers a junction where cyclists can choose between a serene riverside path or delve into the historical wonders of the town center. The choice is yours to make!

7. Junction 6: Szczecin

- As you approach Szczecin, this final junction introduces cyclists to the city's vibrant ambiance. Dive into its cultural offerings and take a well-deserved break before concluding your exhilarating journey.

These key junctions are thoughtfully placed to enhance your cycling experience on the Oder-Neiße Radweg, not only guiding you along the way but also inviting you to immerse yourself in diverse landscapes and cultural treasures that await. Embrace each juncture at your own pace, allowing yourself to unravel the unique allure of every location along this remarkable route.

Here are some suggested accommodations along the route:
1. Starting Point: Zittau, Germany
   - Hotel Stadt Zittau is located at Neustadt 28, 02763 Zittau, Germany. You can contact them at +49 3583 79690. For more information, you can visit their website [here](https://hotel-stadt-zittau.de/).
   - Dresdner Hof Zittau is another option located at Bahnhofstraße 9, 02763 Zittau, Germany. Their telephone number is +49 3583 79060. To find out more about the hotel, you can visit their website [here](https://www.dresdnerhof-zittau.de/).
2. Junction 1: Oder-Neiße Confluence
   - Hotel Oderblick is situated at Wiesenweg 3, 15295 Brieskow-Finkenheerd, Germany. Their telephone number is +49 33603 403. You can find additional details on their website [here](https://www.hotel-oderblick.de/).
   - Another option is Hotel Am Mühlenfließ located at Ziltendorfer Niederung 7, 15299 Müllrose, Germany. You can reach them at +49 33606 6970. For more information about the hotel, you can visit their website [here](https://www.hotel-muehlenfliess.de/).
3. Junction 2: Görlitz
   - Hotel Schwibbogen Görlitz is situated at Struvestr.1,02826 Görlitz, Germany.You may contact them at+49
     ,+49358142190.To know more about the hotel,you may visit their website [here](https://www.schreibers-gasthof.de/).
   - Another option is Hotel Silesia located at Platz des 17. Juni 10,02826 Görlitz, Germany.You can reach them at+49
     ,+49358142190.For more information about the hotel,you may visit their website [here](https://www.hotel-silesia.de/).
4. Junction 3: Bridge Crossing to Poland
   - Hotel Bastion is situated at Ulica Księdza Jerzego Popiełuszki 1,59-301 Luban, Poland.You may contact them at
     +48-75-7825000.For more information about the hotel,you can visit their website [here](https://www.hotelbastion.pl/).

   - Another option is Hotel Restauracja Remes located at Rynek 10,59-300 Luban, Poland.You can reach them at+48-75-7812334.To find out more about the hotel,you can visit their website [here](http://hotelremes.pl/).

Here are some hotel recommendations for each junction along the Oder-Neiße Radweg, ensuring a comfortable and rejuvenating stay for cyclists:

5. Junction 4: Świnoujście

- Hotel Hampton by Hilton Świnoujście is located at Wojska Polskiego 14-16, 72-600 Świnoujście, Poland. You can reach them at +48 91 359 90 00. Visit their website [here](https://www.hilton.com/en/hotels/swihu-hampton-swinoujscie/).

- Hotel Interferie Medical SPA Świnoujście is situated at Ul. Wojska Polskiego 14, 72-600 Świnoujście, Poland. For inquiries, contact them at +48 91 321 71 00. More information can be found on their website [here](https://www.interferie.pl/en).

6. Junction 5: Ueckermünde

- Hotel am Markt is located at Markt 3, 17373 Ueckermünde, Germany. Feel free to call them at +49 39771 5570 or visit their website [here](https://www.hotel-am-markt-ueckermuende.de/).

- HafenHotel PommernYacht can be found at Am Yachthafen8 ,17373 Ueckermünde, Germany. Contact them via telephone at +49 39771 21560 or check out their website [here](https://www.pommetryacht.de/).

7. Junction6: Szczecin

- Hotel Dana Business & Conference is situated at Ul.Krasińskiego14 ,70 -206 Szczecin ,Poland. Get in touch with them by calling +48 91 810 00 00 or visiting their website [here](https://danahotel.pl/en/).

- Hotel Zamek Centrum is located at Ul.Potulicka1 ,70 -255 Szczecin, Poland. You can reach them at +48 91 829 70 70. Find more details on their website [here](http://www.hotelzamek.pl/en/).

These hotel recommendations are carefully selected to ensure a pleasant and comfortable stay for cyclists along the Oder-Neiße

Radweg. Please note that contact information and websites may change, so it's advisable to verify details before planning your stay.

45

Mobile navigation apps play a crucial role in enhancing the cycling experience for those exploring the beautiful Oder-Neiße Radweg. These apps provide real-time navigation, route tracking, and useful information to ensure a seamless journey. Here are some highly recommended mobile navigation apps specifically tailored for cyclists:

1. Komoot
  - Key Features:
    - Detailed Cycling Maps: Komoot offers meticulously designed maps exclusively for cyclists, highlighting bike-friendly routes and important points of interest.
    - Turn-by-Turn Voice Navigation: Enjoy a hands-free experience with turn-by-turn voice guidance, allowing you to fully immerse yourself in the scenic surroundings.
    - Offline Maps: Download maps for offline use, ensuring uninterrupted navigation even in areas with limited cellular connectivity.
    - Elevation Profiles: Gain valuable insights into the terrain with elevation profiles, helping you prepare for challenging uphill climbs and thrilling downhill descents.
  - Availability: Available for both [iOS](https://apps.apple.com/us/app/komoot/id447374873) and [Android](https://play.google.com/store/apps/details?id=de.komoot.android).

2. Strava
  - Key Features:
    - Record Cycling Routes: Strava allows you to effortlessly record your cycling routes, providing comprehensive statistics on distance covered, speed achieved, and elevation gained.
    - Community Features: Connect with fellow cyclists, join vibrant clubs, and proudly share your achievements within the enthusiastic Strava community.

- Segments and Challenges: Push your limits by conquering popular cycling segments and actively participating in exciting monthly challenges.

- Route Planning: Seamlessly plan your cycling route in advance and confidently explore new areas while relying on Strava's reliable guidance.

- Availability: Available for both [iOS](https://apps.apple.com/us/app/strava-run-ride-swim/id426826309) and [Android](https://play.google.com/store/apps/details?id=com.strava).

3. Google Maps

  - Key Features:

    - Bike-Friendly Routes: Google Maps offers cycling-specific routes, providing directions optimized for cyclists, including bike lanes and scenic trails.

    - Offline Maps: Download maps for offline use and navigate without the need for constant internet connectivity, ensuring uninterrupted exploration.

    - Points of Interest: Discover fascinating nearby attractions, delightful restaurants, and convenient repair shops along the captivating Oder-Neiße Radweg.

    - Availability: Pre-installed on most smartphones and can be downloaded on both [iOS](https://apps.apple.com/us/app/google-maps/id585027354) and [Android](https://play.google.com/store/apps/details?id=com.google.android.apps.maps).

4. Bikemap

  - Key Features:

    - Global Cycling Routes: Bikemap provides access to an extensive collection of cycling routes worldwide, including the enchanting Oder-Neiße Radweg.

    - Offline Maps: Download maps to utilize the app offline, ensuring seamless navigation even in areas with weak or no mobile signal.

   - Route Tracking: Capture your thrilling cycling adventures, monitor your performance statistics, and share your remarkable routes with the passionate Bikemap community.
   - Availability: Available for both [iOS](https://apps.apple.com/us/app/bikemap-cycling-map-gps/id989103965) and [Android](https://play.google.com/store/apps/details?id=at.bikemap.android).

When it comes to traveling along the Oder-Neiße Radweg, it's not just about following the path. It's about immersing yourself in the local attractions, services, and hidden gems that you encounter along the way. That's where Local Tourist Information Centers come in. These centers play a vital role in enhancing your cycling experience by providing valuable assistance and insights. Let's take a look at some of the key centers along the Oder-Neiße Radweg:

1. Eisenhüttenstadt Tourist Information
   - Located at Markt 1, 15890 Eisenhüttenstadt, Germany
   - Services offered:
    - Detailed Maps: You can get up-to-date maps of the Oder-Neiße Radweg that highlight key junctions, attractions, and services.
    - Accommodation Information: They can provide recommendations for hotels, guesthouses, and campsites in and around Eisenhüttenstadt.
    - Local Attractions: Discover interesting points of interest, historical sites, and cultural attractions in the Eisenhüttenstadt region.
    - Events and Festivals: Stay informed about local events and festivals happening during your visit.
2. Frankfurt (Oder) Tourist Information
   - Located at Am Damm 51, 15230 Frankfurt (Oder), Germany
   - Services offered:
    - Route Assistance: They can help you plan your cycling route through Frankfurt (Oder) and beyond.
    - Cultural Highlights: Learn about the cultural and historical highlights of Frankfurt (Oder) as well as nearby areas.
    - Dining and Refreshments: Get recommendations for restaurants, cafes, and local eateries along the Oder-Neiße Radweg.

- Practical Information: Inquire about practicalities such as bike repair shops, restrooms, or any other cyclist-friendly facilities.
3. Guben Tourist Information
  - Located at Uferstraße 19, 03172 Guben, Germany
  - Services offered:
  - Border Crossing Information: Receive information about crossing the Oder River into Poland and any related regulations.
  - Multilingual Assistance: Benefit from the assistance of multilingual staff who can communicate in German, English, and Polish.
  - Souvenirs and Maps: You can purchase souvenirs and additional maps to complement the official route information.
  - Emergency Contacts: Obtain local emergency contact numbers and information to ensure a safe journey.
4. Forst (Lausitz) Tourist Information
  - Located at Lindenstraße 10, 03149 Forst (Lausitz), Germany
  - Services offered:
  - Regional Highlights: Explore the highlights of Forst (Lausitz) and gather information about nearby attractions.
  - Accommodation Recommendations: Get suggestions for accommodations based on your preferences and budget.
  - Public Transport Information: Inquire about public transport options available for cyclists and their bikes.
  - Nature and Parks: Learn about scenic spots, parks, and natural attractions in the Forst (Lausitz) region.
These Tourist Information Centers are invaluable resources for cyclists embarking on the Oder-Neiße Radweg. They not only provide practical information but also offer insights into the rich cultural heritage and natural beauty of the regions through which the cycle path winds. So be sure to make a pit stop at these centers to make the most out of your cycling adventure.